THE TARANTULAS

BY
WILLIAM R. SANFORD
CARL R. GREEN

EDITED BY
DR. HOWARD SCHROEDER, Ph.D.
**Professor in Reading and Language Arts
Dept. of Curriculum and Instruction
Mankato State University**

CRESTWOOD HOUSE
Mankato, Minnesota

CIP

LIBRARY OF CONGRESS CATALOGING IN PUBLICATION DATA

Sanford, William R. (William Reynolds).
 The tarantulas.
 (Wildlife, habits & habitat)
 Includes index.
 SUMMARY: Describes the physical characteristics, habits, natural
environment, and relationship to humans of the tarantula, one of a group
of spiders whose size and weight makes it impossible for them to spin a
web strong enough to hold them.
 1. Tarantulas--Juvenile literature. (1. Tarantulas. 2. Spiders.) I. Green,
Carl R. II. Schroeder, Howard. III. Title. IV. Series.
QL458.42.T5S26 1987   595.4'4   87-22342
ISBN 0-89686-339-5

International Standard Book Number:	**Library of Congress Catalog Card Number:**
Library Binding 0-89686-339-5	87-22342

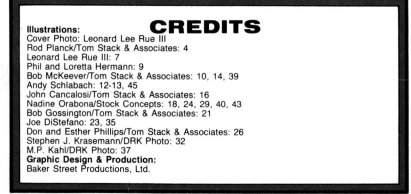

CREDITS

Illustrations:
Cover Photo: Leonard Lee Rue III
Rod Planck/Tom Stack & Associates: 4
Leonard Lee Rue III: 7
Phil and Loretta Hermann: 9
Bob McKeever/Tom Stack & Associates: 10, 14, 39
Andy Schlabach: 12-13, 45
John Cancalosi/Tom Stack & Associates: 16
Nadine Orabona/Stock Concepts: 18, 24, 29, 40, 43
Bob Gossington/Tom Stack & Associates: 21
Joe DiStefano: 23, 35
Don and Esther Phillips/Tom Stack & Associates: 26
Stephen J. Krasemann/DRK Photo: 32
M.P. Kahl/DRK Photo: 37
Graphic Design & Production:
Baker Street Productions, Ltd.

CRESTWOOD HOUSE

Hwy. 66 South, Box 3427
Mankato, MN 56002-3427

TABLE OF CONTENTS

Introduction 5
    The biggest spider I've ever seen!
Chapter One: The tarantula in close-up 8
    What is a tarantula?
    Big enough to be scary
    The tarantula's body: the cephalothorax
    The tarantula's body: the legs and abdomen
    Limited senses get the job done
    A weird and successful animal
Chapter Two: The tarantula sticks
close to its burrow 19
    Building a snug burrow
    Some tarantulas don't fit the pattern
    Tarantulas are patient hunters
    Molting gives a fresh start
    Predators and other dangers
Chapter Three: The tarantula's life cycle 27
    The tarantulas mate
    Making an egg sac and laying eggs
    The spiderlings hatch
    Going out to live — and die
    Completing the cycle
Chapter Four: Tarantulas aren't as
bad as people think 34
    The tarantula attracts myths
    Dealing with the tarantula's poison
    Danger! Watch tarantulas on duty!
Chapter Five: A tarantula makes
an interesting pet 40
    Tarantulas aren't scary after all
    A tarantula needs a good home
    Molting can be exhausting
    An unusual pet-show entry
Map: 45
Index/Glossary: 46-47

Many people are surprised when they learn that tarantulas are not insects.

INTRODUCTION:

"Are you ready for your tour?" the guide asked. "I'm Ms. Perez. Welcome to the Natural History Museum."

Joe and Laura shook hands with their guide. This tour was their prize for winning first place in the school Science Fair. Ms. Perez had arranged to show them the rooms where the scientists worked.

"Follow me," Ms. Perez told them. She unlocked a door and led them into a big room filled with lab equipment.

"This is exciting!" Laura said. She pointed to a glass tank that stood on a nearby table. "What's that fish tank doing here? It doesn't have any water in it."

"Come over and meet Snoopy," Ms. Perez replied.

Laura looked into the tank. "Good grief!" she gasped. "That's the biggest, ugliest insect I've ever seen."

"Don't hurt Snoopy's feelings," Ms. Perez said with a smile. "I don't think he's ugly, and he's certainly not an insect."

Joe studied the ten-inch (25 cm) creature. "I know," he said at last. "Snoopy is a tarantula, isn't he? That means he's a spider. But aren't spiders insects?"

"Yes and no," Ms. Perez said. "Yes, Snoopy is a South American bird-eating tarantula. The *Guinness*

Book of World Records says that Snoopy and his cousins are the world's biggest spiders. But no, spiders aren't insects."

"As far as I'm concerned, all creepy-crawly things are insects," Laura said. She was a little afraid of Snoopy. As she watched, the tarantula moved across the bottom of his tank. His hairy legs moved slowly.

"Look carefully and you'll see why Snoopy is a spider and not an insect," Ms. Perez said. "First, spiders have eight legs. Insects have six. Second, a spider's body is made up of two main parts. There's a combined head and chest, and then there's the abdomen. An insect's body has three parts. The head and the chest are separate."

"Are those the only differences?" Joe asked.

"That's only a start," Ms. Perez replied. "Many of the differences relate to the fact that spiders are more primitive than insects. Spiders don't have antennae (feelers) on their heads, but insects do. A tarantula has eight eyes, but it doesn't see very well. An insect's eyes are made up of hundreds of light-sensitive cells. It sees very well. Finally, a spider's lungs are much simpler than an insect's lungs. Snoopy has four slits in his abdomen. Inside his body, air passes over folds of tissue that hang down like the pages of a book. The blood that flows through these 'book lungs' absorbs oxygen from the air."

"I won't call spiders insects again," Laura promised. She bent down to take a closer look at Snoopy.

6

Unlike insects, tarantulas do not have feelers.

"A friend of my dad's keeps tarantulas as pets," Joe said. "Maybe he'll sell one to me."

"Tarantulas make interesting pets," Ms. Perez agreed. "But I think you should learn more about them before you buy one. At the end of your visit, I'll loan each of you a book about tarantulas."

Ms. Perez looked at her watch. "Now, say goodbye to Snoopy. We've got a lot to see before the museum closes."

CHAPTER ONE:

Imagine that every animal in the world has been lined up by size. The line would stretch all the way from the great blue whale to a crowd of tiny, almost invisible creatures. Three out of four animals in the line would come from the phylum *Arthropoda*. These are the animals with jointed legs and external skeletons—crabs, lobsters, centipedes, insects, and spiders. The animals with backbones may be larger, but the arthropods outnumber them.

What is a tarantula?

Naturalists give every living creature a name that tells about its place in nature. Spiders are arthropods, but that's a very general name. To be more specific, they belong to the class known as the *Arachnida*. The arachnids include scorpions, mites, and ticks, as well as spiders. Within the arachnids, all spiders are placed in the order *Araneae*. Next, naturalists divide the *Araneae* into primitive spiders and true spiders. The suborder *Mygalomorphae* contains the large, heavy-bodied, primitive spiders. Most mygalomorphs live in underground burrows because they can't spin a web strong enough to hold them. The spiders called tarantulas are members of this suborder.

This striped-tail scorpion is a "cousin" to the tarantula.

Tarantulas have been around for thousands of years. In that time, they've adapted to many different habitats. By one count, there are at least 1,500 species of tarantulas living in warm climates around the world. In the Americas, tarantulas can be found in the southwestern United States, Mexico, Central America, and much of South America. True tarantulas don't live east of the Mississippi River.

Latin Americans often call tarantulas "hairy spiders." The name fits!

The United States has about thirty species of tarantulas. Most belong to the family *Theraphosidae*. By rights, they shouldn't be called tarantulas at all. The original tarantula is the wolf spider of southern Europe, *Lycosa narbonensis*. It's too late to change the name now, but wolf spiders and tarantulas are very different. Perhaps it would be more accurate to use the tarantula's Spanish name. In Latin America, tarantulas are often called *arañas peludas*—the hairy spiders.

Big enough to be scary

Tarantulas are easily the biggest of all spiders. The giant bird-eating spider of South America *(Theraphosa leblondii)* has a three-and-a-half-inch (9 cm) body. Its legs span a distance of ten inches (25 cm). A mature male has longer legs than a female, but the female is heavier. A full-grown female of this species can weigh up to three ounces (85 grams).

The tarantula of the American Southwest is smaller, but it's still big enough to scare people. A male tarantula *(Dugesiella hentzi)* has a two-inch (5 cm) body and a leg span of seven inches (18 cm). A large Dugesiella female weighs two-thirds of an ounce (19 grams) after a good feeding. Some smaller species have bodies as tiny as one-eighth inch (3.2 mm) in length.

The tarantula's body: the cephalothorax

All tarantulas are heavy-bodied, hairy spiders. The front half of their two-part body is called the cephalothorax. The back half is the abdomen. The cephalothorax contains the tarantula's brain, nervous system, sucking stomach, eyes, fangs, and mouth.

Two fang-tipped chelicerae extend downward beside the tarantula's mouth. The chelicerae act almost like a pair of jaws, holding prey while the spider is eating. When the tarantula hunts, it leaps on its prey and plunges its half-inch (1.3 cm) fangs into the body. Then the fangs pump poison into the prey. The tarantula also uses its chelicerae for digging.

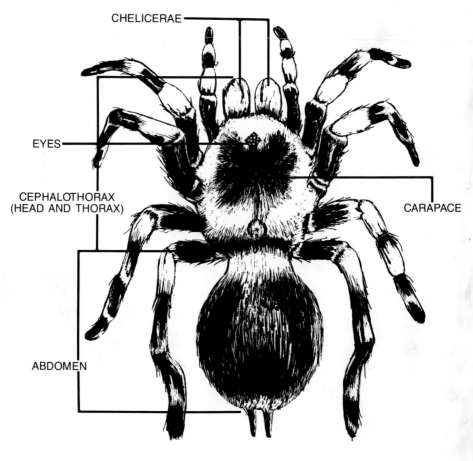

CHELICERAE

EYES

CEPHALOTHORAX
(HEAD AND THORAX)

CARAPACE

ABDOMEN

TOP VIEW

A pair of arm-like pedipalpi grow beside the chelicerae. These useful limbs are almost as long as the tarantula's legs. The tarantula uses the pedipalpi as feelers to help it locate prey. They're also good for carrying food to the spider's mouth. Finally, the male stores his sperm in the tips of the pedipalpi before he leaves his burrow to find a mate.

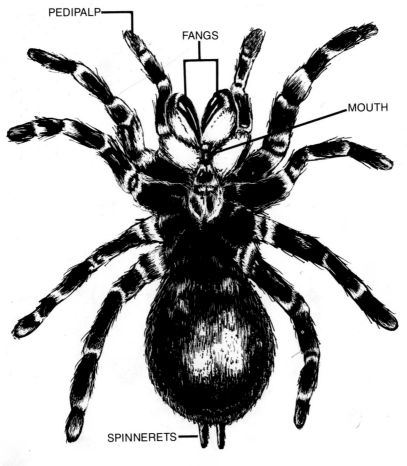

PEDIPALP

FANGS

MOUTH

SPINNERETS

BOTTOM VIEW

Tarantulas have a pair of claws on each leg.

The cephalothorax is protected by a hard shell called the carapace. In different species, the carapace varies in color from purple to dark brown to a greenish-black. Some tarantulas, such as the Mexican red-leg, have bands of bright color on their legs. Others have splashes of color on the carapace. Fine hair grows all over the tarantula, but it's longest on the abdomen and legs.

The tarantula's body: the legs and abdomen

The tarantula's legs connect to the cephalothorax at a spot called the apodeme. With so many legs, the tarantula can move quickly in any direction. It's not much of a leaper, however. When it's hunting crickets, the tarantula's best jump is only a few inches. Each hairy leg is tipped with two claws. The claws, along with a set of sticky hairs at the end of each leg, let the tarantula climb almost anywhere. Some South American tarantulas have left the ground to make their homes in trees.

The abdomen is the bulb-shaped structure behind the cephalothorax. Here are found the tarantula's digestive tube, heart, book lungs, reproductive system, and four spinnerets. The spinnerets, which stick out from the tarantula's tail like tiny nozzles, spin the liquid silk into webs. The liquid flows from a gland inside the abdomen. The spinnerets form the quick-hardening silk into a thread.

Along with lining its burrow, the female tarantula uses the silk to make egg sacs. Some tarantulas also weave a "doormat" that traps insects in front of their burrows. The prey's struggle alerts the tarantula to the dinner that's waiting outside.

A mole cricket makes a tasty dinner for this tarantula.

Limited senses get the job done

Naturalists are still learning about the tarantula's senses. They do know that the spider has eight eyes, located just above its mouth. Even with eight eyes, however, a tarantula can't see objects more than a few inches away. A grasshopper can be sitting quietly a foot (30 cm) away and the tarantula won't know it's there.

In order to hunt, the tarantula depends on its well-developed sense of touch. The body hairs act as sensors to detect movement and vibrations. Because the tarantula depends on movement to identify its prey, it will pass up an animal that isn't moving. Some naturalists think these big spiders also have a sense of hearing. Scientists base this idea on the fact that one species of Texas tarantula makes a barking noise.

The tarantula's senses include taste and smell. Caged tarantulas will turn down cockroaches and other insects that don't taste good. More important to the nearly blind tarantula are the white lyre organs on the underside of its legs. These organs are the spider's odor detectors. During the mating season, males "home in" on the female's scent from a mile (1.6 km) or more away.

A weird and successful animal

Put all these parts together, and you have the tarantula. It may be weird looking, but it's one of nature's best designs. If you know where to look, and if you're patient, you can see one in its wild habitat. That's where naturalists go when they want to study this large, hairy spider.

Most North American tarantulas live in semi-desert areas.

CHAPTER TWO:

Most tarantulas prefer a warm climate without too much rain. In the United States, many tarantulas live in the states of Nevada, New Mexico, Arizona, and Texas. They aren't limited to those states, however. Naturalists find tarantula burrows as far east as the Mississippi River and as far west as California.

Tarantulas dig their burrows on open hillsides or amid the scrub growth of semi-desert regions. Grassy areas near plowed fields are another favorite. By and large, tarantulas stay out of thick forests and heavy brush. The tree-living tarantulas of South America's rain forests are the exceptions to that rule. Naturalists think that heavy rains drove these tarantulas out of their burrows and into the trees.

Building a snug burrow

Tarantulas usually dig their own burrows. If they move into a mouse or snake burrow, they remodel it to suit themselves. Once established, they may stay in that same burrow for many years. If a tarantula is digging its own burrow, it tunnels straight down for about ten inches (25 cm). The spider then curves its tunnel parallel with the ground. At the end of the tunnel it digs a snug den. As the tarantula grows, it enlarges the hole with its fangs and "wallpapers" the burrow with a layer of silk.

A tarantula spends much of its time below ground. Except when fleeing from floods or predators, the spider comes out only to hunt or to mate. Some species build a circular mound of grass at the burrow's entrance. Here they sit and wait for a bug to stray within range. Other tarantulas wait for their prey to step on the silk "doormat" they spin outside the burrow.

It's not unusual for a colony of tarantulas to live within a few feet of one another. That could be dangerous, because tarantulas will sometimes eat one another. But these spiders are so short-sighted they probably never know the others are there.

Some tarantulas don't fit the pattern

The tarantula family includes three small spiders that have unusual habits. Naturalists call them the atypical tarantulas. They generally live farther north than do the *Theraphosidae,* and several live in the eastern United States.

The trapdoor spider *(Aliatypus californicus)* caps its tunnels with doors that fit like a cork. This spider can hold its door closed against any insect enemy. But when a bug walks by, the tarantula pops out and pulls in its dinner.

By contrast, the purse-web spider *(Atypus abboti)* digs a tunnel about two feet (61 cm) deep. Then it weaves a silk tube that extends six to eight inches (15 to 20 cm) above the tunnel. The spider often props the tube against a tree trunk for support. When an insect lands on it, the spider dashes up the inside of the tube. Then it opens a hole and grabs its victim.

Finally, the funnel-web tarantula *(Euagrus comstocki)* lives up to its name. It spins a funnel-shaped web, with the mouth of its burrow at the center. The web is anchored by supports that reach out to nearby rocks or roots. The funnel attracts insects, which become easy prey for the waiting spider.

A tarantula's patience is rewarded with a big grasshopper.

Tarantulas are patient hunters

Most North American tarantulas feed on insects. They're patient hunters who wait for the prey to come to them. When it does, they're quick enough to catch a moth on the wing. Tarantulas also eat beetles, sowbugs, millipedes, crickets, and grasshoppers. The larger tarantulas add small frogs, mice, lizards, and birds to their diet.

Despite their size, tarantulas aren't big eaters. In captivity, a large tarantula stays healthy on four or five crickets a week. In the winter, the spider may go for several months without eating. In one experiment, a female tarantula lived for twenty-eight months without food.

The tarantula uses its hollow fangs to inject its poison. Small animals die quickly, but a tarantula bite can kill larger animals as well. A mole, for example, died thirty-six hours after being bitten. The poison also softens the tissues of the victim's body. That allows the tarantula to suck the fluids out with its fangs. When the tarantula is finished, a dead insect looks like a dried-up piece of skin.

Molting gives a fresh start

Young tarantulas shed their old skins two to four times a year. This process is called molting. If they

When a tarantula molts, it replaces worn or missing body parts— including legs!

23

didn't molt, they wouldn't have room to grow. Each new shell is larger than the one before. Molting also allows the tarantula to replace worn and missing parts. A tarantula that loses a leg will grow a new one!

After they reach maturity at eight to ten years, the spiders molt only once a year. Until that time, it's almost impossible to tell a male from a female. When the mature male steps out of his old skin, he reveals brighter colors and longer legs than the female. The male now goes looking for a mate. Whether he finds one or not, he'll die within a year.

Male tarantulas usually have brighter colors and longer legs than females. Shown above is a Mexican red-leg.

Although it drinks extra water, a tarantula does not eat for two weeks before molting. To start the process, it spins a soft "molting bed" on the floor of its burrow. Then the spider lays on its back and wiggles its legs to loosen the old skin. Next, it turns on its side and climbs out of the old skin. The old skin comes off in one piece. The entire process can take an entire day, and leaves the tarantula worn out.

The tarantula lies quietly while the new skin hardens. These first hours are critical. If the skin breaks, the tarantula will bleed to death. There are other dangers as well. Any insect that invades the burrow can attack the helpless spider. In addition, some spiders never do get their legs free. They die tangled up in their old skins.

Predators and other dangers

Tarantulas stay well hidden, but predators do find them. Digging animals such as the skunk, wild pig, and coatimundi enjoy a snack of tarantula, large or small. When young tarantulas leave the burrow, they face an army of predators that includes birds, lizards, frogs, toads, and snakes. The young ones sometimes eat other young tarantulas.

A few smaller insects also prey on the tarantula. Ants sometimes swarm into a burrow and destroy an egg sac. A fly of the family *Acroceridae* lays its eggs on the tarantula's body. As the maggots hatch, they feast on their walking dinner plate. Even more deadly is the

25

With so many predators and dangers around, a tarantula's life is never easy.

Pepsis wasp. This wasp paralyzes the tarantula and lays its egg under the helpless spider's body. When the egg hatches, the larva eats the spider alive.

Accidents kill more tarantulas. Males go out to find females and are squashed by autos when they cross a road. A farmer plows a field and buries a hundred tarantula burrows. Hard rains can flood the burrows, and drought can drive away the insects the tarantula needs for food.

If they survive the first year, female tarantulas sometimes live up to twenty-five years. The males die after they reach maturity around their tenth year. It is the female who hatches the spiderlings that begin each new life cycle.

CHAPTER THREE:

Fall is turning the first leaves to gold in an Arkansas woodland. Two children walk down a quiet hillside, talking and laughing. They don't notice the life that is stirring in the tarantula burrows on the hill.

A ten-year-old male tarantula molted two weeks ago. His bright colors show that he is mature and ready to mate. This morning, he deposits his sperm on a silk sheet that he had spun earlier. Later, he fills the bulbs on the end of his pedipalpi with sperm. Then he's ready to look for a female.

The tarantulas mate

As the male tarantula wanders away from his burrow, the breeze plays across the lyre organs under his legs. The scent he's searching for isn't there. Driven by instinct, he moves across rocks and under bushes. The world beyond the next few inches is nothing but vague, blurry shadows. At last, he finds a tarantula burrow where the scent is right. The female that lives here is ready to mate. The male taps on the web that covers the entrance. Nothing happens. He taps out a rhythm with his forelegs.

Suddenly, the web that covers the hole splits open. The female's long, brown legs emerge, then her head. The male strokes her legs. The vibration seems to put her into a trance. When she's quiet, he moves forward. The female rears up on her back legs. Her fangs point at the male, but he's ready for this. He pins down her fangs with the hooks that grow under his forelegs. Then he places his sperm in the mating slits on her abdomen with his pedipalpi.

As soon as the mating is over, the female is ready to attack. If she could catch the male, she'd likely kill him. This time, the male backs away quickly and escapes. When the mating season ends, his spinnerets will drop off and his hair will fall out in patches. He'll die before the next molt.

The female retreats into her burrow. She's well fed after a summer of good hunting. When the weather turns cold, she plugs up the entrance and settles down for the winter. She won't lay her eggs until spring.

Making an egg sac and laying eggs

April brings warmer weather. The tarantula opens the sealed entrance and catches a June bug almost at once. She fills herself with food. She'll need plenty of energy for the hard labor of spinning an egg sac and laying her eggs.

Male tarantulas lose their hair in patches after they mate.

A week later, the female is ready. She goes inside her burrow and starts work. Fifteen hours later, the first step is finished. She's spun a silken pad that measures just less than three inches (7.6 cm) by five inches (12.7 cm). The pad is soft enough and strong enough to protect her eggs.

After she rests awhile, the female lays her first yellow-green egg. From then on, she lays two eggs every three seconds until she has more than six hundred eggs. Some females lay as few as sixty eggs, and others lay more than a thousand. The eggs have soft skins that harden quickly.

When the female is finished laying, she spins another sheet to lay over the eggs. Then she forms the entire bundle into an egg sac and seals it with more silk. The egg sac looks like a lumpy round purse. Instinct tells the tarantula that she must not leave it for even a minute. She climbs up on the egg sac and begins her six weeks of guard duty.

The spiderlings hatch

The female carefully guards her egg sac. Most insect predators back away when they see her. Her biggest threat comes from a nearby nest of red ants. The ants have already invaded another burrow. There they swarmed over the female and forced her to flee. She left the egg sac behind, to be ripped open by the ants.

On sunny days, the nesting tarantula drags the egg sac outside. Carefully, she turns each side to the warm sun. The female keeps two or three legs on the egg sac at all times. When she senses danger, she pops the sac back into the burrow.

The spiderlings hatch in three weeks, but they stay in the egg sac for another three weeks. When they finally break out of the sac, the young tarantulas are only a sixth of an inch (4.2 mm) long. Except for their white skins, they look like tiny adults. Soon, hundreds of tiny tarantulas are swarming around the burrow. The female joins her young in spinning a nest that will serve as a nursery. The best-developed spiderlings are already growing. They molt their first skins at the end of the week.

Going out to live – and die

Within two weeks, all of the spiderlings have left the burrow. Most travel only a few yards before they duck into safe hiding places under rocks and in small holes. For the most part, they're too small to catch their own food. Many won't eat until the following spring.

Only the strongest spiderlings survive that first year. The lucky ones find ready-made burrows. Others dig

A young tarantula looks for a place to hide from predators.

their own. Many are snapped up by birds and lizards. During the summer, a rainstorm drowns some more. That winter, snow and ice take their toll of the survivors. Toward the end of the cold weather, the remaining spiderlings are driven by a terrible hunger. A few make it through to spring by eating their brothers and sisters.

In April, a skunk digs down to the female's burrow. The tarantula defends herself in an unusual way. She scrapes hairs from her abdomen and flicks them at the skunk. The cloud of hair stings the predator's eyes and nose. The skunk backs away, sneezing and pawing at its eyes.

The female digs a new burrow, only to face another danger. A female Pepsis wasp stalks into the burrow. The tarantula stands up tall and strikes at her smaller enemy. The wasp easily avoids the deadly fangs and stings the spider again and again. The poison paralyzes the tarantula—but doesn't kill her.

The wasp drags the tarantula to her own hole. There, she lays a single egg and glues it to the spider's abdomen. Then the wasp covers the spider with dirt before she flies away. Because the tarantula is alive, she won't decay. Thus, when the egg hatches, the wasp larva will have fresh food.

Completing the cycle

The surviving spiderlings grow slowly into adults. They feed, molt, and wait out the winters in their burrows. In ten years, the males will be ready to mate. The females won't mature until two years later. The hillside colony is doing well—until workers bring in bulldozers to build a new road. No one worries about killing a few dozen tarantulas.

CHAPTER FOUR:

Many people have never seen a tarantula, nor do they want to see one. They've learned about tarantulas by watching films.

The tarantulas that appear in movies are usually deadly killers. In the James Bond thriller, *Dr. No,* the spy barely escapes the bite of a "poisonous" tarantula. The sight of the huge spider crawling toward the sleeping Bond gave nightmares to adults and children alike. Similarly, in *Kiss of the Tarantula,* a girl keeps tarantulas in her cellar. She uses them to kill off her uncle, stepmother, and school classmates.

The facts about tarantulas clearly deny these colorful fictions. But a thousand people may see a film like *Dr. No* for every person who sees a nature film about tarantulas.

The tarantula's name and reputation come from the southern Italian seaport of Taranto. There, in the 1400's, people often saw large wolf spiders in the fields. *Tarantula* was the local name for these spiders. A legend grew up that tarantulas hunted people. In truth, spiders would never chase a human being, but people believed the legend.

The story didn't stop there. The natives said that people bitten by tarantulas would die unless they took

Tarantulas aren't the deadly killers that appear in movies—but they still are fascinating creatures!

the "dancing cure." Musicians were called in to play their pipes and fiddles. Then the victims began to dance. They danced slowly at first, then faster and faster. The frenzy lasted until the weary dancers fell to the ground, cured.

People also believed that others could "catch" the fever. There was nothing for them to do but join the dance. In this way, entire villages soon were dancing. The rapid, whirling steps became a popular folk dance called the tarantella. Historians remind us that the church had strict laws against dancing in the 1400's. Thus, the first tarantella may have been a clever way to get around church rules.

The tarantula attracts myths

The tarantula appears in other folk myths as well. Natives in Central America believe that a tarantula bite causes a horse's hoof to fall off. The local name for the tarantula is "horse killer." On the island of Jamaica, children learn about a clever god who is half human and half tarantula. The myth probably doesn't mean much to these children, who have never seen a tarantula.

In parts of Asia, people eat tarantulas as snacks!

In 1872, sugarcane planters brought in mongooses to hunt the island's rats. The mongooses controlled the rats, but they also wiped out the island's tarantulas.

In Malaysia, a large tarantula is thought to be a god. When people pray to this tarantula, they call it "Earth Tiger." The Malaysian spider is lucky. Elsewhere in southeast Asia, people use the tarantula as a snack food.

Dealing with the tarantula's poison

North American Indians turned to plants to find a cure for the tarantula's poison. The Navahos drank a medicinal tea brewed from the bladderpod plant. The nearby Hopi Indians rubbed the skin around a bite with wild sunflowers. Farther north, the Blackfoot soaked a cloth in juice from the western wood lily and wrapped it around the wound.

In truth, the bite of most tarantulas is no more dangerous than a bee sting. The larger South American tarantulas can do more harm, but they're seldom seen in the United States. The biggest danger is that the person bitten may be allergic to the poison. These are the same people who go into shock when they're bitten by a bee. Similarly, some tarantulas are quick to flick their abdomenal hairs when they're bothered. The hairs can cause a painful eye irritation or a skin rash.

In nature, tarantulas hide when people come anywhere near them. Therefore, it's safe to say that most bites happen when people corner a tarantula or try to pick it up. In the same way, captive tarantulas don't like to be handled too much. If they're hungry, or if it's mating season, they may strike at anyone holding them.

Most tarantula stings are no worse than the sting of a bee.

Danger! Watch tarantulas on duty!

A jewelry store in San Francisco suffered from a number of burglaries. The security system wasn't working, so a new plan was tried. The owners rented tarantulas and put them in the jewelry cases at night. On the front door, they posted a sign that read: "This store patrolled by tarantulas." The robberies stopped at once.

Tarantula security systems are rare. But some people do keep them as pets. That's an interesting way to learn about this largest of all the spiders.

CHAPTER FIVE:

Jim Kazak watched as the girl entered his pet store. This was her fifth visit in the past week. If he was reading the signs right, she was ready to buy something.

"May I help you?" he asked.

The girl turned quickly. "Hi, Mr. Kazak. I'm Caroline Lake. I've come to buy one of your tarantulas," she said.

Red-legged tarantulas may be bought in pet stores for around fifteen dollars (US).

Tarantulas aren't scary after all

Mr. Kazak always checked to see that his animals were going to good homes. Did Caroline really want a tarantula? "Most girls would be afraid of a tarantula," he said.

"Not me," Caroline said proudly. "A friend of mine has a tarantula, so I know how to handle them. And my parents say I can have one if I take good care of it."

"You know more about tarantulas than most people," Mr. Kazak said with a smile. "How would you like to hold Pedro?" He picked up a Honduran black velvet tarantula and put it on the girl's hand. The spider tried to crawl away, but Caroline had her other hand waiting to catch him.

"Easy, big fellow," Caroline said to Pedro. "One good fall could kill you." Pedro turned and crawled up her arm.

"How does it feel to have Pedro walking on your arm?" Mr. Kazak asked.

"He tickles a little, but he's as light as a feather," she said. "I think he's beautiful! How much does he cost?"

"Pedro is a prize specimen," Mr. Kazak said as he put the tarantula back in his tank. "He costs fifty dollars (US). I have some young Mexican red-legs that are only fifteen dollars. Do you have a tarantularium for your pet?"

A tarantula needs a good home

"I've fixed up an old five-gallon (19 liter) fish tank," Caroline replied. "I cleaned it and put aquarium gravel in the bottom. My friend told me not to use dirt from the yard, because it might carry parasites. I'm using an ashtray as a water dish."

"Good!" Mr. Kazak said. "You can build a burrow out of rocks. And be sure to put a lid on the tank. Tarantulas can climb straight up a glass wall. Finally, keep the temperature above seventy degrees Fahrenheit (22 degrees C). These are warm-weather animals. What are you going to feed your tarantula?"

"I'll catch crickets and sowbugs and other insects," Caroline said. "I know that tarantulas need live food. But what will I do in the winter if I can't find any insects?"

"I sell crickets and mealy worms here in the store," Mr. Kazak told her. "In a pinch, you could feed your tarantula a small goldfish, or even hamburger."

Caroline looked confused. "He wouldn't eat hamburger, would he? I thought—"

"You'd have to trick him," Mr. Kazak explained. "Put some hamburger around a piece of thread. Place the meat near the tarantula and jerk the thread to make it move. Some tarantulas can be fooled into thinking it's alive. Keep tugging on the thread until the tarantula

If handled with care, tarantulas can make interesting pets!

has eaten. But don't worry if your pet refuses to eat. Tarantulas never overeat, and they often go weeks without food during the winter.''

Molting can be exhausting

"That sounds like good advice," Caroline said. "Can you tell me what I should do when my tarantula molts?"

"One of my Mexican red-legs molted last week,"
Mr. Kazak said. "I gave her plenty of water ahead of
time, and she slipped out of her old skin without any
trouble. Most of the time, the molting goes smoothly,
but it does tire the animal. Don't handle the tarantula
for a week or so afterward."

"Well, I guess I'm ready to pick out my tarantula,"
Caroline said. "I'd like to buy Pedro, but I don't have
that much money. So, I'll take one of the young ones.
Can I have a female?"

"I'll do my best," Mr. Kazak said, "but these spiders
are only two years old. Males and females look very
much alike until the male's final molt. Anyway, the
males do everything the females do, except lay eggs."

An unusual pet-show entry

"One last thing," Caroline said. "Can I show my
tarantula at pet shows?"

"Some people will scream," Mr. Kazak laughed,
"but I've won blue ribbons with my tarantulas. The
biggest problem is finding an official who knows how
to judge a tarantula."

"Thanks, Mr. Kazak," Caroline said excitedly.
"Now, give me the biggest red-leg you have. I can't
wait to see the look on my mom's face when I take it
home!"

MAP:

The North American
tarantulas are found
within the shaded areas.
Tarantulas are also found
in much of South America.

45

INDEX/GLOSSARY:

ABDOMEN 6, 11, 14, 15, 28, 33, 38 — *The bulb-shaped rear half of a spider's two-part body. The abdomen contains the spider's heart, lungs, digestive tube, reproductive system, and spinnerets.*

BEHAVIOR 11, 12, 13, 15, 20, 21, 27, 28

BOOK LUNGS 6, 15 — *The tarantula's primitive lungs, in which air passes over folds of tissue that look like the pages of a book.*

BURROW 8, 13, 15, 19, 20, 21, 25, 26, 27, 28, 30, 31, 32, 33, 42 — *The hole where a tarantula lives and molts, and in which the female hatches her young.*

CARAPACE 14 — *The hard plate that covers the upper surface of a tarantula's cephalothorax.*

CEPHALOTHORAX 11, 14, 15 — *The front half of a spider's two-part body. The legs are attached to the cephalothorax, as are the chelicerae and the pedipalpi.*

CHELICERAE 12, 13 — *Two jaw-like bodies that contain the tarantula's fangs. The chelicerae are located just below the spider's eyes.*

COLOR 14, 24, 27, 31

DIET 17, 21, 22, 25, 42

EGG SAC 15, 25, 28, 30, 31 — *The silk bag that the female tarantula spins to protect her eggs until the spiderlings are hatched.*

ENEMIES 20, 25, 26, 30, 31, 32, 33

FANGS 11, 12, 20, 22, 28, 33 — *Sharp, hollow teeth that the tarantula uses to inject poison into its prey.*

HABITAT 9, 18, 19 — *The place where an animal makes its home.*

INSTINCTS 27, 30 — *Behaviors an animal follows automatically from the time it's born.*

LYRE ORGANS 17, 27 — *Openings on the underside of the legs that give the tarantula its sense of smell.*

MATING 17, 27, 28

MOLTING 22, 24, 25, 27, 28, 31, 33, 43, 44 — *When a tarantula sheds its old skin.*

MYTHS 34, 36 — *Beliefs that people hold even though they run counter to the laws of nature.*

NATURALIST 8, 17, 18, 19, 20 — *A scientist who studies animal and plant life.*

INDEX/GLOSSARY:

PEDIPALPI 13, 27, 28 — *Two limbs located next to the chelicerae that serve as the tarantula's "arms."*

PHYSICAL CHARACTERIS-TICS 6, 11, 14, 15, 22

PREDATORS 20, 25, 26, 30, 33 — *Animals that live by preying on other animals.*

PRIMITIVE 6, 8 — *When an animal's body or behavior is less developed than that of other similar animals.*

SENSES 6, 17

SIZE 11, 31

SPERM 13, 27 — *The male sex cells that fertilize the female's eggs.*

SPIDERLING 26, 30, 31, 32, 33 — *A newly hatched male or female tarantula.*

SPINNERETS 15, 28 — *The rear-facing tubes that the tarantula uses to spin its liquid silk into a thread.*

TARANTULARIUM 41 — *A container that has been set up as a home for a pet tarantula.*

WEIGHT 11, 31

47

WILDLIFE

HABITS & HABITAT

READ AND ENJOY THE SERIES:

If you would like to know more about all kinds of wildlife, you should take a look at the other books in this series.

You'll find books on bald eagles and other birds. Books on alligators and other reptiles. There are books about deer and other big-game animals. And there are books about sharks and other creatures that live in the ocean.

In all of the books you will learn that life in the wild is not easy. But you will also learn what people can do to help wildlife survive. So read on!